CHURCH MUSIC SOCIETY REPRINTS No. 75
Honorary General Editor: Richard Lyne

FOUR MOTETS

Mass Propers for the Feast of All Saints

by

WILLIAM BYRD

(1543-1623)

Introit: Gaudeamus omnes
Gradual: Timete Dominum
Offertory: Justorum animae
Communion: Beati mundo corde

Edited by Sally Dunkley

Published for the
CHURCH MUSIC SOCIETY
by
OXFORD UNIVERSITY PRESS
WALTON STREET OXFORD OX2 6DP

Source

Gradualia ac cantiones sacrae (London, 1605), nos 29-32, 'In festo omnium Sanctorum'

Editorial note

The music has been transposed down a tone. Editorial material is shown in small type or within square brackets. Italic type indicates editorial word underlay prompted by a repeat sign in the original. Though the term 'versus' (Introit, bar 43 and Gradual, bar 26) refers to the structure of the word text rather than the music, it may be thought appropriate to perform these sections with reduced forces. An approximate metronome speed is given at the start of each piece, but this is no more than an editorial suggestion.

Texts

The texts form the Propers of the Mass for the Feast of All Saints, celebrated on 1 November.

Introit

Let us all rejoice in the Lord and keep a festival in honour of all the saints. Let us join with the angels in joyful praise to the Son of God. *Ps*. Ring out your joy to the Lord, O you just; for praise is fitting for loyal hearts. Glory be to the Father and to the Son and to the Holy Spirit, as it was in the beginning, is now, and ever shall be, world without end. Amen. [*D.C.*]

Gradual & Alleluia

Revere the Lord, you his saints. They lack nothing, those who revere him. ℣. Those who seek the Lord lack no blessing. Alleluia. Come to me, all you who labour and are overburdened, and I will give you rest. Alleluia.

Offertory

The souls of the righteous are in the hands of God, no torment of death shall ever touch them. In the eyes of the unwise, they did appear to die, but they are in peace.

Communion

Happy are the pure of heart for they shall see God. Happy are the peacemakers; they shall be called sons of God. Happy are they who suffer persecution for the sake of justice; the kingdom of heaven is theirs.

Sally Dunkley
London, 1992

Mass Propers
for the Feast of All Saints

William Byrd (1543–1623)
edited by Sally Dunkley

1 Introit

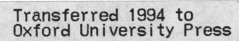

4

30

gau – dent an – ge – li, gau – dent an – ge-li, gau-

an – ge-li, gau – dent an – ge-li, gau – dent an – ge-li,

– dent an – ge-li, an – ge-li, gau-dent an – ge-li, gau – dent

gau – dent an – ge-li, an – ge – li, an – ge – li, gau –

gau – – dent an – ge – li, gau – dent

– dent an-ge-li, an – ge – li, et col – lau – dant,

et col – lau – dant, et col – lau – dant, et col –

an – ge – li, et col-lau – dant, et col-lau –

– dent an – ge – li, et col-lau – dant, et col-lau – dant,

an – ge – li, et col-lau – dant, et col-lau –

8

[Fine]

De — — — — — — — — — **i.**

— **i, Fi** — **li** — **um De** — — — **i.**

Fi — *li* — *um De* — — — *i.*

— [i, **Fi** — **li** — **um De-**] — **i.**

— — — — — — — — — **i.**

Versus
S.2

45

Ex — **ul** –**ta** – **te,** **ex** – **ul** –**ta** – **te** **ju** – **sti** **in**

A.

Ex – **ul** –**ta** – **te,** **ex** – **ul** –**ta** — **te** **ju** – **sti**

T.

Ex – **ul** –**ta** – **te** **ju** – **sti** **in** **Do** – **mi** –**no,** **in**

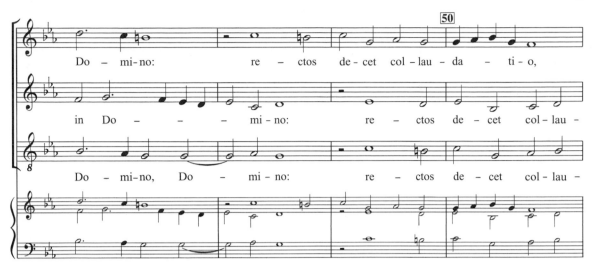

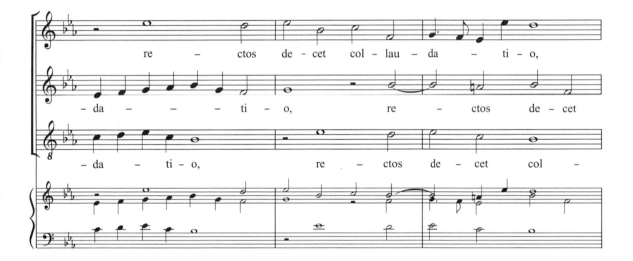

10

[Repeat bars 1–42]

2 Gradual & Alleluia

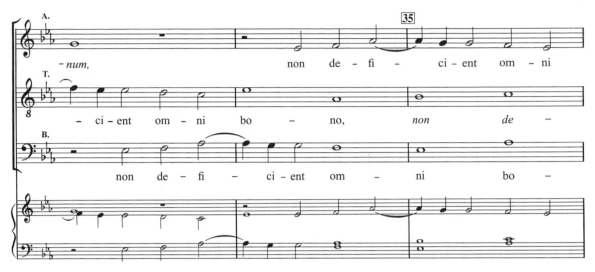

la — bo — ra — tis, la — bo — ra — tis, qui
— bo — ra — tis, *qui la — bo — ra*
qui la — bo — ra — — tis —
la — bo — ra — tis, qui la — bo — ra — tis,

60

la — bo — ra — tis, et o — ne — ra — ti
— *tis,* et o — ne — ra — ti e —
— *tis, qui la — bo — ra — tis,* la-bo — ra —
qui la — bo — ra — tis, la-bo — ra — tis,____

qui la-bo-ra — tis,____

28

3 Offertory

34

4 Communion

42